Wall Street News Network
Stock Trading Journal

Copyright 2019 Wall Street News Network Publishing
All rights reserved
https://WStNN.com

Stock Trading Quotations

Only enter a trade after the action of the market confirms your opinion and then enter promptly.
~ Jesse Livermore

A great stock, though with small profits, generally increases faster than a small stock with great profits.
~ Adam Smith

The stock market is a no-called-strike game. You don't have to swing at everything — you can wait for your pitch
~ Warren Buffett

Basically, what I do is place a stop, generally 10 to 20 percent below the current price, whenever I buy a stock. The exact level depends on my own analysis of a stock's trading pattern. If a stock violates this stop, I'm out.
~ Martin Zweig

Buy rising stocks and sell falling stocks.
~ Jesse Livermore

There were a few penny-mining-stock brokerage firms doing business with the outside world. Here was an opportunity for the great American speculating public to take "a flyer" on something much more tangible and lasting than a horse-race.
~ George Graham Rice, 1911

Do not trade every day of every year.
~ Jesse Livermore

"The men on the trading floor may not have been to school, but they have Ph.D.'s in man's ignorance."
~ Michael M. Lewis

"Trader has to reverse what you might call his natural impulses. Instead of hoping he must fear; instead of fearing he must hope.
~ Jesse Lauriston Livermore

"There is a saying that bad traders divorce their spouse sooner than abandon their positions. Loyalty to ideas is not a good thing for traders, scientists - or anyone."
~ Nassim Nicholas Taleb

"I just wait until there is money lying in the corner, and all I have to do is go over there and pick it up. I do nothing in the meantime."
~ Jim Rogers

"The market is a device for transferring money from the impatient to the patient."
~ Warren Buffet

"The market can stay irrational longer than you can stay solvent."
~ John Maynard Keynes

"Hope is bogus emotion that only costs you money."
~ Jim Cramer

Date: _____

Symbol: _____   Company: _____

Opening Transaction

Transaction Recommended By

Why decision was made to do this transaction

Buy/Short	# of Shares	Price/share	Commission	Subtotal

Total opening transaction _____

Closing Transaction

Why decision was made to close at this price

Sell/cover	# of Shares	Price/share	Commission	Subtotal

Total closing transaction _____

Overall Profit/Loss _____

What I learned from this transaction

Date: _____

Symbol: _____   Company:_____

Opening Transaction

Transaction Recommended By

Why decision was made to do this transaction

Buy/Short	# of Shares	Price/share	Commission	Subtotal

Total opening transaction

Closing Transaction

Why decision was made to close at this price

Sell/cover	# of Shares	Price/share	Commission	Subtotal

Total closing transaction

Overall Profit/Loss

What I learned from this transaction

Date: _____

Symbol: _____   Company: _____

Opening Transaction

Transaction Recommended By _____

Why decision was made to do this transaction

Buy/Short	# of Shares	Price/share	Commission	Subtotal

Total opening transaction   [   ]

Closing Transaction

Why decision was made to close at this price

Sell/cover	# of Shares	Price/share	Commission	Subtotal

Total closing transaction   [   ]

Overall Profit/Loss   [   ]

What I learned from this transaction

Date: _____

Symbol: _____   Company: _____

Opening Transaction

Transaction Recommended By
_____

Why decision was made to do this transaction

Buy/Short	# of Shares	Price/share	Commission	Subtotal

Total opening transaction   [_____]

Closing Transaction

Why decision was made to close at this price

Sell/cover	# of Shares	Price/share	Commission	Subtotal

Total closing transaction   [_____]

Overall Profit/Loss   [_____]

What I learned from this transaction

Date: _____

Symbol: _____   Company: _____

Opening Transaction
Transaction Recommended By _____

Why decision was made to do this transaction

Buy/Short	# of Shares	Price/share	Commission	Subtotal

Total opening transaction [   ]

Closing Transaction
Why decision was made to close at this price

Sell/cover	# of Shares	Price/share	Commission	Subtotal

Total closing transaction [   ]

Overall Profit/Loss [   ]

What I learned from this transaction

Date: _____

Symbol: _____   Company:_____

Opening Transaction

Why decision was made to do this transaction

Buy/Short	# of Shares	Price/share	Commission	Subtotal

Total opening transaction _____

Closing Transaction

Why decision was made to close at this price

Sell/cover	# of Shares	Price/share	Commission	Subtotal

Total closing transaction _____

Overall Profit/Loss _____

What I learned from this transaction

Date: _____

Symbol: _____   Company: _____

Opening Transaction

Transaction Recommended By

Why decision was made to do this transaction

Buy/Short	# of Shares	Price/share	Commission	Subtotal

Total opening transaction

Closing Transaction

Why decision was made to close at this price

Sell/cover	# of Shares	Price/share	Commission	Subtotal

Total closing transaction

Overall Profit/Loss

What I learned from this transaction

Date: _____

Symbol: _____   Company: _____

Opening Transaction
Transaction Recommended By _____

Why decision was made to do this transaction

Buy/Short	# of Shares	Price/share	Commission	Subtotal

Total opening transaction ☐

Closing Transaction
Why decision was made to close at this price

Sell/cover	# of Shares	Price/share	Commission	Subtotal

Total closing transaction ☐

Overall Profit/Loss ☐

What I learned from this transaction

Date: _____

Symbol: _____   Company: _____

Opening Transaction

Transaction Recommended By
_____

Why decision was made to do this transaction

Buy/Short	# of Shares	Price/share	Commission	Subtotal

Total opening transaction _____

Closing Transaction

Why decision was made to close at this price

Sell/cover	# of Shares	Price/share	Commission	Subtotal

Total closing transaction _____

Overall Profit/Loss _____

What I learned from this transaction

Date: _____

Symbol: _____   Company: _____

Opening Transaction

Transaction Recommended By _____

Why decision was made to do this transaction

Buy/Short	# of Shares	Price/share	Commission	Subtotal

Total opening transaction ☐

Closing Transaction

Why decision was made to close at this price

Sell/cover	# of Shares	Price/share	Commission	Subtotal

Total closing transaction ☐

Overall Profit/Loss ☐

What I learned from this transaction

Date: _____

Symbol: _____   Company: _____

Opening Transaction

Transaction Recommended By _____

Why decision was made to do this transaction

Buy/Short	# of Shares	Price/share	Commission	Subtotal

Total opening transaction [_____]

Closing Transaction

Why decision was made to close at this price

Sell/cover	# of Shares	Price/share	Commission	Subtotal

Total closing transaction [_____]

Overall Profit/Loss [_____]

What I learned from this transaction

Date: _____

Symbol: _____   Company: _____

Opening Transaction

Transaction Recommended By

Why decision was made to do this transaction

Buy/Short	# of Shares	Price/share	Commission	Subtotal

Total opening transaction _____

Closing Transaction

Why decision was made to close at this price

Sell/cover	# of Shares	Price/share	Commission	Subtotal

Total closing transaction _____

Overall Profit/Loss _____

What I learned from this transaction

Date: _____

Symbol: _____   Company: _____

Opening Transaction
Transaction Recommended By _____

Why decision was made to do this transaction

Buy/Short	# of Shares	Price/share	Commission	Subtotal

Total opening transaction

Closing Transaction
Why decision was made to close at this price

Sell/cover	# of Shares	Price/share	Commission	Subtotal

Total closing transaction

Overall Profit/Loss

What I learned from this transaction

Date: _____

Symbol: _____   Company: _____

Opening Transaction

Transaction Recommended By

Why decision was made to do this transaction

Buy/Short	# of Shares	Price/share	Commission	Subtotal

Total opening transaction _____

Closing Transaction

Why decision was made to close at this price

Sell/cover	# of Shares	Price/share	Commission	Subtotal

Total closing transaction _____

Overall Profit/Loss _____

What I learned from this transaction

Date: _____

Symbol: _____   Company: _____

Opening Transaction

Why decision was made to do this transaction

Buy/Short	# of Shares	Price/share	Commission	Subtotal

Total opening transaction _____

Closing Transaction

Why decision was made to close at this price

Sell/cover	# of Shares	Price/share	Commission	Subtotal

Total closing transaction _____

Overall Profit/Loss _____

What I learned from this transaction

Date: _____

Symbol: _____   Company: _____

Opening Transaction
Transaction Recommended By

Why decision was made to do this transaction

Buy/Short	# of Shares	Price/share	Commission	Subtotal

Total opening transaction _____

Closing Transaction
Why decision was made to close at this price

Sell/cover	# of Shares	Price/share	Commission	Subtotal

Total closing transaction _____

Overall Profit/Loss _____

What I learned from this transaction

Date: _____

Symbol: _____   Company: _____

Opening Transaction

Transaction Recommended By _____

Why decision was made to do this transaction

Buy/Short	# of Shares	Price/share	Commission	Subtotal

Total opening transaction ☐

Closing Transaction

Why decision was made to close at this price

Sell/cover	# of Shares	Price/share	Commission	Subtotal

Total closing transaction ☐

Overall Profit/Loss ☐

What I learned from this transaction

Date: _____

Symbol: _____   Company: _____

Opening Transaction

Transaction Recommended By

Why decision was made to do this transaction

Buy/Short	# of Shares	Price/share	Commission	Subtotal

Total opening transaction [_____]

Closing Transaction

Why decision was made to close at this price

Sell/cover	# of Shares	Price/share	Commission	Subtotal

Total closing transaction [_____]

Overall Profit/Loss [_____]

What I learned from this transaction

Date: _____

Symbol: _____   Company: _____

Opening Transaction

Transaction Recommended By _____

Why decision was made to do this transaction

Buy/Short	# of Shares	Price/share	Commission	Subtotal

Total opening transaction [____]

Closing Transaction

Why decision was made to close at this price

Sell/cover	# of Shares	Price/share	Commission	Subtotal

Total closing transaction [____]

Overall Profit/Loss [____]

What I learned from this transaction

Date: _____

Symbol: _____   Company: _____

Opening Transaction

Transaction Recommended By

Why decision was made to do this transaction

Buy/Short	# of Shares	Price/share	Commission	Subtotal

Total opening transaction _____

Closing Transaction

Why decision was made to close at this price

Sell/cover	# of Shares	Price/share	Commission	Subtotal

Total closing transaction _____

Overall Profit/Loss _____

What I learned from this transaction

Date: _____

Symbol: _____ Company: _____

Opening Transaction
Transaction Recommended By _____

Why decision was made to do this transaction

Buy/Short	# of Shares	Price/share	Commission	Subtotal

Total opening transaction _____

Closing Transaction
Why decision was made to close at this price

Sell/cover	# of Shares	Price/share	Commission	Subtotal

Total closing transaction _____

Overall Profit/Loss _____

What I learned from this transaction

Date: _____

Symbol: _____   Company: _____

Opening Transaction
Transaction Recommended By

Why decision was made to do this transaction

Buy/Short	# of Shares	Price/share	Commission	Subtotal

Total opening transaction _____

Closing Transaction
Why decision was made to close at this price

Sell/cover	# of Shares	Price/share	Commission	Subtotal

Total closing transaction _____

Overall Profit/Loss _____

What I learned from this transaction

Date: _____

Symbol: _____   Company: _____

Opening Transaction

Transaction Recommended By

Why decision was made to do this transaction

Buy/Short	# of Shares	Price/share	Commission	Subtotal

Total opening transaction [_____]

Closing Transaction

Why decision was made to close at this price

Sell/cover	# of Shares	Price/share	Commission	Subtotal

Total closing transaction [_____]

Overall Profit/Loss [_____]

What I learned from this transaction

Date: _____

Symbol: _____   Company: _____

Opening Transaction

Transaction Recommended By _____

Why decision was made to do this transaction

Buy/Short	# of Shares	Price/share	Commission	Subtotal

Total opening transaction _____

Closing Transaction

Why decision was made to close at this price

Sell/cover	# of Shares	Price/share	Commission	Subtotal

Total closing transaction _____

Overall Profit/Loss _____

What I learned from this transaction

Date: _____

Symbol: _____   Company:_____

Opening Transaction
Transaction Recommended By

Why decision was made to do this transaction

Buy/Short	# of Shares	Price/share	Commission	Subtotal

Total opening transaction _____

Closing Transaction
Why decision was made to close at this price

Sell/cover	# of Shares	Price/share	Commission	Subtotal

Total closing transaction _____

Overall Profit/Loss _____

What I learned from this transaction

Date: _____

Symbol: _____   Company: _____

Opening Transaction

Transaction Recommended By

Why decision was made to do this transaction

Buy/Short	# of Shares	Price/share	Commission	Subtotal

Total opening transaction _____

Closing Transaction

Why decision was made to close at this price

Sell/cover	# of Shares	Price/share	Commission	Subtotal

Total closing transaction _____

Overall Profit/Loss _____

What I learned from this transaction

Date: _____

Symbol: _____   Company: _____

Opening Transaction
Transaction Recommended By
_____

Why decision was made to do this transaction

_____

Buy/Short	# of Shares	Price/share	Commission	Subtotal

Total opening transaction _____

Closing Transaction
Why decision was made to close at this price

_____

Sell/cover	# of Shares	Price/share	Commission	Subtotal

Total closing transaction _____

Overall Profit/Loss _____

What I learned from this transaction

_____

Date: _____

Symbol: _____   Company: _____

Opening Transaction
Transaction Recommended By

Why decision was made to do this transaction

Buy/Short	# of Shares	Price/share	Commission	Subtotal

Total opening transaction _____

Closing Transaction
Why decision was made to close at this price

Sell/cover	# of Shares	Price/share	Commission	Subtotal

Total closing transaction _____

Overall Profit/Loss _____

What I learned from this transaction

Date: _____

Symbol: _____   Company: _____

Opening Transaction

Transaction Recommended By

Why decision was made to do this transaction

Buy/Short	# of Shares	Price/share	Commission	Subtotal

Total opening transaction

Closing Transaction

Why decision was made to close at this price

Sell/cover	# of Shares	Price/share	Commission	Subtotal

Total closing transaction

Overall Profit/Loss

What I learned from this transaction

Date: _____

Symbol: _____   Company: _____

Opening Transaction
Transaction Recommended By

Why decision was made to do this transaction

Buy/Short	# of Shares	Price/share	Commission	Subtotal

Total opening transaction ☐

Closing Transaction
Why decision was made to close at this price

Sell/cover	# of Shares	Price/share	Commission	Subtotal

Total closing transaction ☐

Overall Profit/Loss ☐

What I learned from this transaction

Date: _____

Symbol: _____   Company: _____

Opening Transaction

Transaction Recommended By
_____

Why decision was made to do this transaction

Buy/Short	# of Shares	Price/share	Commission	Subtotal

Total opening transaction _____

Closing Transaction

Why decision was made to close at this price

Sell/cover	# of Shares	Price/share	Commission	Subtotal

Total closing transaction _____

Overall Profit/Loss _____

What I learned from this transaction

Date: _____

Symbol: _____   Company: _____

Opening Transaction
Transaction Recommended By

Why decision was made to do this transaction

Buy/Short	# of Shares	Price/share	Commission	Subtotal

Total opening transaction

Closing Transaction
Why decision was made to close at this price

Sell/cover	# of Shares	Price/share	Commission	Subtotal

Total closing transaction

Overall Profit/Loss

What I learned from this transaction

Date: _____

Symbol: _____   Company:_____

Opening Transaction
Transaction Recommended By

Why decision was made to do this transaction

Buy/Short	# of Shares	Price/share	Commission	Subtotal

Total opening transaction

Closing Transaction
Why decision was made to close at this price

Sell/cover	# of Shares	Price/share	Commission	Subtotal

Total closing transaction

Overall Profit/Loss

What I learned from this transaction

Date: _____

Symbol: _____   Company: _____

Opening Transaction
Transaction Recommended By

Why decision was made to do this transaction

Buy/Short	# of Shares	Price/share	Commission	Subtotal

Total opening transaction _____

Closing Transaction
Why decision was made to close at this price

Sell/cover	# of Shares	Price/share	Commission	Subtotal

Total closing transaction _____

Overall Profit/Loss _____

What I learned from this transaction

Date: _____

Symbol: _____   Company:_____

Opening Transaction
Transaction Recommended By

Why decision was made to do this transaction

Buy/Short	# of Shares	Price/share	Commission	Subtotal

Total opening transaction

Closing Transaction
Why decision was made to close at this price

Sell/cover	# of Shares	Price/share	Commission	Subtotal

Total closing transaction

Overall Profit/Loss

What I learned from this transaction

Date: _____

Symbol: _____   Company: _____

Opening Transaction

Transaction Recommended By _____

Why decision was made to do this transaction

Buy/Short	# of Shares	Price/share	Commission	Subtotal

Total opening transaction [   ]

Closing Transaction

Why decision was made to close at this price

Sell/cover	# of Shares	Price/share	Commission	Subtotal

Total closing transaction [   ]

Overall Profit/Loss [   ]

What I learned from this transaction

Date: _____

Symbol: _____   Company: _____

Opening Transaction
Transaction Recommended By _____

Why decision was made to do this transaction

Buy/Short	# of Shares	Price/share	Commission	Subtotal

Total opening transaction

Closing Transaction
Why decision was made to close at this price

Sell/cover	# of Shares	Price/share	Commission	Subtotal

Total closing transaction

Overall Profit/Loss

What I learned from this transaction

Date: _____

Symbol: _____   Company: _____

Opening Transaction
Transaction Recommended By _____

Why decision was made to do this transaction

Buy/Short	# of Shares	Price/share	Commission	Subtotal

Total opening transaction _____

Closing Transaction
Why decision was made to close at this price

Sell/cover	# of Shares	Price/share	Commission	Subtotal

Total closing transaction _____

Overall Profit/Loss _____

What I learned from this transaction

Date: _____

Symbol: _____   Company: _____

Opening Transaction

Transaction Recommended By _____

Why decision was made to do this transaction

Buy/Short	# of Shares	Price/share	Commission	Subtotal

Total opening transaction _____

Closing Transaction

Why decision was made to close at this price

Sell/cover	# of Shares	Price/share	Commission	Subtotal

Total closing transaction _____

Overall Profit/Loss _____

What I learned from this transaction

Date: _____

Symbol: _____   Company: _____

Opening Transaction

Why decision was made to do this transaction

Buy/Short	# of Shares	Price/share	Commission	Subtotal

Total opening transaction _____

Closing Transaction

Why decision was made to close at this price

Sell/cover	# of Shares	Price/share	Commission	Subtotal

Total closing transaction _____

Overall Profit/Loss _____

What I learned from this transaction

Date: _____

Symbol: _____   Company: _____

Opening Transaction
Transaction Recommended By

Why decision was made to do this transaction

Buy/Short	# of Shares	Price/share	Commission	Subtotal

Total opening transaction

Closing Transaction
Why decision was made to close at this price

Sell/cover	# of Shares	Price/share	Commission	Subtotal

Total closing transaction

Overall Profit/Loss

What I learned from this transaction

Date: _____

Symbol: _____ Company: _____

Opening Transaction

Transaction Recommended By

Why decision was made to do this transaction

Buy/Short	# of Shares	Price/share	Commission	Subtotal

Total opening transaction _____

Closing Transaction

Why decision was made to close at this price

Sell/cover	# of Shares	Price/share	Commission	Subtotal

Total closing transaction _____

Overall Profit/Loss _____

What I learned from this transaction

Date: _____

Symbol: _____   Company: _____

Opening Transaction

Transaction Recommended By _____

Why decision was made to do this transaction

Buy/Short	# of Shares	Price/share	Commission	Subtotal

Total opening transaction [_____]

Closing Transaction

Why decision was made to close at this price

Sell/cover	# of Shares	Price/share	Commission	Subtotal

Total closing transaction [_____]

Overall Profit/Loss [_____]

What I learned from this transaction

Date: _____

Symbol: _____   Company: _____

Opening Transaction

Transaction Recommended By

Why decision was made to do this transaction

Buy/Short	# of Shares	Price/share	Commission	Subtotal

Total opening transaction [_____]

Closing Transaction

Why decision was made to close at this price

Sell/cover	# of Shares	Price/share	Commission	Subtotal

Total closing transaction [_____]

Overall Profit/Loss [_____]

What I learned from this transaction

Date: _____

Symbol: _____   Company:_____

Opening Transaction

Transaction Recommended By _____

Why decision was made to do this transaction

Buy/Short	# of Shares	Price/share	Commission	Subtotal

Total opening transaction _____

Closing Transaction

Why decision was made to close at this price

Sell/cover	# of Shares	Price/share	Commission	Subtotal

Total closing transaction _____

Overall Profit/Loss _____

What I learned from this transaction

Date: _____

Symbol: _____   Company: _____

Opening Transaction

Transaction Recommended By
_____

Why decision was made to do this transaction

Buy/Short	# of Shares	Price/share	Commission	Subtotal

Total opening transaction _____

Closing Transaction

Why decision was made to close at this price

Sell/cover	# of Shares	Price/share	Commission	Subtotal

Total closing transaction _____

Overall Profit/Loss _____

What I learned from this transaction

Date: _____

Symbol: _____   Company: _____

Opening Transaction

Transaction Recommended By

Why decision was made to do this transaction

Buy/Short	# of Shares	Price/share	Commission	Subtotal

Total opening transaction _____

Closing Transaction

Why decision was made to close at this price

Sell/cover	# of Shares	Price/share	Commission	Subtotal

Total closing transaction _____

Overall Profit/Loss _____

What I learned from this transaction

Date: _____

Symbol: _____ Company: _____

Opening Transaction

Transaction Recommended By _____

Why decision was made to do this transaction

Buy/Short	# of Shares	Price/share	Commission	Subtotal

Total opening transaction ⬜

Closing Transaction

Why decision was made to close at this price

Sell/cover	# of Shares	Price/share	Commission	Subtotal

Total closing transaction ⬜

Overall Profit/Loss ⬜

What I learned from this transaction

Date: _____

Symbol: _____   Company: _____

Opening Transaction
Transaction Recommended By _____

Why decision was made to do this transaction

Buy/Short	# of Shares	Price/share	Commission	Subtotal

Total opening transaction

Closing Transaction
Why decision was made to close at this price

Sell/cover	# of Shares	Price/share	Commission	Subtotal

Total closing transaction

Overall Profit/Loss

What I learned from this transaction

Date: _____

Symbol: _____   Company: _____

Opening Transaction

Transaction Recommended By

Why decision was made to do this transaction

Buy/Short	# of Shares	Price/share	Commission	Subtotal

Total opening transaction

Closing Transaction

Why decision was made to close at this price

Sell/cover	# of Shares	Price/share	Commission	Subtotal

Total closing transaction

Overall Profit/Loss

What I learned from this transaction

Date: _____

Symbol: _____   Company: _____

Opening Transaction

Transaction Recommended By
_____

Why decision was made to do this transaction

Buy/Short	# of Shares	Price/share	Commission	Subtotal

Total opening transaction [_____]

Closing Transaction

Why decision was made to close at this price

Sell/cover	# of Shares	Price/share	Commission	Subtotal

Total closing transaction [_____]

Overall Profit/Loss [_____]

What I learned from this transaction

Date: _____

Symbol: _____   Company: _____

Opening Transaction
Transaction Recommended By

Why decision was made to do this transaction

Buy/Short	# of Shares	Price/share	Commission	Subtotal

Total opening transaction _____

Closing Transaction
Why decision was made to close at this price

Sell/cover	# of Shares	Price/share	Commission	Subtotal

Total closing transaction _____

Overall Profit/Loss _____

What I learned from this transaction

Date: _____

Symbol: _____   Company: _____

Opening Transaction

Transaction Recommended By

Why decision was made to do this transaction

Buy/Short	# of Shares	Price/share	Commission	Subtotal

Total opening transaction

Closing Transaction

Why decision was made to close at this price

Sell/cover	# of Shares	Price/share	Commission	Subtotal

Total closing transaction

Overall Profit/Loss

What I learned from this transaction

Date: _____

Symbol: _____   Company: _____

Opening Transaction
Transaction Recommended By
_____

Why decision was made to do this transaction
_____

Buy/Short	# of Shares	Price/share	Commission	Subtotal

Total opening transaction _____

Closing Transaction
Why decision was made to close at this price
_____

Sell/cover	# of Shares	Price/share	Commission	Subtotal

Total closing transaction _____

Overall Profit/Loss _____

What I learned from this transaction
_____

Date: _____

Symbol: _____   Company: _____

Opening Transaction
Transaction Recommended By _____

Why decision was made to do this transaction

Buy/Short	# of Shares	Price/share	Commission	Subtotal

Total opening transaction

Closing Transaction
Why decision was made to close at this price

Sell/cover	# of Shares	Price/share	Commission	Subtotal

Total closing transaction

Overall Profit/Loss

What I learned from this transaction

Date: _____

Symbol: _____   Company: _____

Opening Transaction

Transaction Recommended By

Why decision was made to do this transaction

Buy/Short	# of Shares	Price/share	Commission	Subtotal

Total opening transaction

Closing Transaction

Why decision was made to close at this price

Sell/cover	# of Shares	Price/share	Commission	Subtotal

Total closing transaction

Overall Profit/Loss

What I learned from this transaction

Date: _____

Symbol: _____   Company: _____

Opening Transaction

Transaction Recommended By

Why decision was made to do this transaction

Buy/Short	# of Shares	Price/share	Commission	Subtotal

Total opening transaction

Closing Transaction

Why decision was made to close at this price

Sell/cover	# of Shares	Price/share	Commission	Subtotal

Total closing transaction

Overall Profit/Loss

What I learned from this transaction

Date: _____

Symbol: _____   Company: _____

Opening Transaction
Transaction Recommended By _____

Why decision was made to do this transaction

Buy/Short	# of Shares	Price/share	Commission	Subtotal

Total opening transaction _____

Closing Transaction
Why decision was made to close at this price

Sell/cover	# of Shares	Price/share	Commission	Subtotal

Total closing transaction _____

Overall Profit/Loss _____

What I learned from this transaction

Date: _____

Symbol: _____   Company: _____

Opening Transaction
Transaction Recommended By

Why decision was made to do this transaction

Buy/Short	# of Shares	Price/share	Commission	Subtotal

Total opening transaction _____

Closing Transaction
Why decision was made to close at this price

Sell/cover	# of Shares	Price/share	Commission	Subtotal

Total closing transaction _____

Overall Profit/Loss _____

What I learned from this transaction

Date: _____

Symbol: _____   Company: _____

Opening Transaction

Transaction Recommended By

Why decision was made to do this transaction

Buy/Short	# of Shares	Price/share	Commission	Subtotal

Total opening transaction

Closing Transaction

Why decision was made to close at this price

Sell/cover	# of Shares	Price/share	Commission	Subtotal

Total closing transaction

Overall Profit/Loss

What I learned from this transaction

Date: _____

Symbol: _____   Company: _____

Opening Transaction

Transaction Recommended By
_____

Why decision was made to do this transaction

Buy/Short	# of Shares	Price/share	Commission	Subtotal

Total opening transaction

Closing Transaction

Why decision was made to close at this price

Sell/cover	# of Shares	Price/share	Commission	Subtotal

Total closing transaction

Overall Profit/Loss

What I learned from this transaction

Date: _____

Symbol: _____   Company: _____

Opening Transaction
Transaction Recommended By _____

Why decision was made to do this transaction

Buy/Short	# of Shares	Price/share	Commission	Subtotal

Total opening transaction

Closing Transaction
Why decision was made to close at this price

Sell/cover	# of Shares	Price/share	Commission	Subtotal

Total closing transaction

Overall Profit/Loss

What I learned from this transaction

Date: _____

Symbol: _____   Company: _____

Opening Transaction

Transaction Recommended By

Why decision was made to do this transaction

Buy/Short	# of Shares	Price/share	Commission	Subtotal

Total opening transaction _____

Closing Transaction

Why decision was made to close at this price

Sell/cover	# of Shares	Price/share	Commission	Subtotal

Total closing transaction _____

Overall Profit/Loss _____

What I learned from this transaction

Date: _____

Symbol: _____   Company: _____

Opening Transaction
Transaction Recommended By

Why decision was made to do this transaction

Buy/Short	# of Shares	Price/share	Commission	Subtotal

Total opening transaction ☐

Closing Transaction
Why decision was made to close at this price

Sell/cover	# of Shares	Price/share	Commission	Subtotal

Total closing transaction ☐

Overall Profit/Loss ☐

What I learned from this transaction

Date: _____

Symbol: _____   Company: _____

Opening Transaction

Transaction Recommended By

Why decision was made to do this transaction

Buy/Short	# of Shares	Price/share	Commission	Subtotal

Total opening transaction

Closing Transaction

Why decision was made to close at this price

Sell/cover	# of Shares	Price/share	Commission	Subtotal

Total closing transaction

Overall Profit/Loss

What I learned from this transaction

Date: _____

Symbol: _____   Company: _____

Opening Transaction
Why decision was made to do this transaction

Why decision was made to do this transaction

Buy/Short	# of Shares	Price/share	Commission	Subtotal

Total opening transaction _____

Closing Transaction
Why decision was made to close at this price

Sell/cover	# of Shares	Price/share	Commission	Subtotal

Total closing transaction _____

Overall Profit/Loss _____

What I learned from this transaction

Date: _____

Symbol: _____   Company: _____

Opening Transaction

Transaction Recommended By _____

Why decision was made to do this transaction

Buy/Short	# of Shares	Price/share	Commission	Subtotal

Total opening transaction _____

Closing Transaction

Why decision was made to close at this price

Sell/cover	# of Shares	Price/share	Commission	Subtotal

Total closing transaction _____

Overall Profit/Loss _____

What I learned from this transaction

Date: _____

Symbol: _____   Company: _____

Opening Transaction
Transaction Recommended By

Why decision was made to do this transaction

Buy/Short	# of Shares	Price/share	Commission	Subtotal

Total opening transaction _____

Closing Transaction
Why decision was made to close at this price

Sell/cover	# of Shares	Price/share	Commission	Subtotal

Total closing transaction _____

Overall Profit/Loss _____

What I learned from this transaction

Date: _____

Symbol: _____   Company: _____

Opening Transaction
Transaction Recommended By

Why decision was made to do this transaction

Buy/Short	# of Shares	Price/share	Commission	Subtotal

Total opening transaction

Closing Transaction
Why decision was made to close at this price

Sell/cover	# of Shares	Price/share	Commission	Subtotal

Total closing transaction

Overall Profit/Loss

What I learned from this transaction

Date: _____

Symbol: _____   Company: _____

Opening Transaction

Transaction Recommended By
_____

Why decision was made to do this transaction

Buy/Short	# of Shares	Price/share	Commission	Subtotal

Total opening transaction _____

Closing Transaction

Why decision was made to close at this price

Sell/cover	# of Shares	Price/share	Commission	Subtotal

Total closing transaction _____

Overall Profit/Loss _____

What I learned from this transaction

Date: _____

Symbol: _____   Company: _____

Opening Transaction
Transaction Recommended By _____

Why decision was made to do this transaction

Buy/Short	# of Shares	Price/share	Commission	Subtotal

Total opening transaction _____

Closing Transaction
Why decision was made to close at this price

Sell/cover	# of Shares	Price/share	Commission	Subtotal

Total closing transaction _____

Overall Profit/Loss _____

What I learned from this transaction

Date: _____

Symbol: _____   Company: _____

Opening Transaction

Transaction Recommended By

Why decision was made to do this transaction

Buy/Short	# of Shares	Price/share	Commission	Subtotal

Total opening transaction _____

Closing Transaction

Why decision was made to close at this price

Sell/cover	# of Shares	Price/share	Commission	Subtotal

Total closing transaction _____

Overall Profit/Loss _____

What I learned from this transaction

Date: _____

Symbol: _____   Company:_____

Opening Transaction

Transaction Recommended By _____

Why decision was made to do this transaction

Buy/Short	# of Shares	Price/share	Commission	Subtotal

Total opening transaction

Closing Transaction

Why decision was made to close at this price

Sell/cover	# of Shares	Price/share	Commission	Subtotal

Total closing transaction

Overall Profit/Loss

What I learned from this transaction

Date: _____

Symbol: _____   Company: _____

Opening Transaction
Transaction Recommended By

Why decision was made to do this transaction

Buy/Short	# of Shares	Price/share	Commission	Subtotal

Total opening transaction _____

Closing Transaction
Why decision was made to close at this price

Sell/cover	# of Shares	Price/share	Commission	Subtotal

Total closing transaction _____

Overall Profit/Loss _____

What I learned from this transaction

Date: _____

Symbol: _____   Company:_____

Opening Transaction

Transaction Recommended By _____

Why decision was made to do this transaction

Buy/Short	# of Shares	Price/share	Commission	Subtotal

Total opening transaction   [   ]

Closing Transaction

Why decision was made to close at this price

Sell/cover	# of Shares	Price/share	Commission	Subtotal

Total closing transaction   [   ]

Overall Profit/Loss   [   ]

What I learned from this transaction

Date: _____

Symbol: _____   Company: _____

Opening Transaction

Transaction Recommended By

Why decision was made to do this transaction

Buy/Short	# of Shares	Price/share	Commission	Subtotal

Total opening transaction _____

Closing Transaction

Why decision was made to close at this price

Sell/cover	# of Shares	Price/share	Commission	Subtotal

Total closing transaction _____

Overall Profit/Loss _____

What I learned from this transaction

Date: _____

Symbol: _____   Company: _____

Opening Transaction
Transaction Recommended By

Why decision was made to do this transaction

Buy/Short	# of Shares	Price/share	Commission	Subtotal

Total opening transaction _____

Closing Transaction
Why decision was made to close at this price

Sell/cover	# of Shares	Price/share	Commission	Subtotal

Total closing transaction _____

Overall Profit/Loss _____

What I learned from this transaction

Date: _____

Symbol: _____   Company: _____

Opening Transaction
Transaction Recommended By
_____

Why decision was made to do this transaction

_____

Buy/Short	# of Shares	Price/share	Commission	Subtotal

Total opening transaction _____

Closing Transaction
Why decision was made to close at this price

_____

Sell/cover	# of Shares	Price/share	Commission	Subtotal

Total closing transaction _____

Overall Profit/Loss _____

What I learned from this transaction

_____

Date: _____

Symbol: _____   Company: _____

Opening Transaction

Transaction Recommended By _____

Why decision was made to do this transaction

Buy/Short	# of Shares	Price/share	Commission	Subtotal

Total opening transaction

Closing Transaction

Why decision was made to close at this price

Sell/cover	# of Shares	Price/share	Commission	Subtotal

Total closing transaction

Overall Profit/Loss

What I learned from this transaction

Date: _____

Symbol: _____   Company: _____

Opening Transaction
Transaction Recommended By

Why decision was made to do this transaction

Buy/Short	# of Shares	Price/share	Commission	Subtotal

Total opening transaction _____

Closing Transaction
Why decision was made to close at this price

Sell/cover	# of Shares	Price/share	Commission	Subtotal

Total closing transaction _____

Overall Profit/Loss _____

What I learned from this transaction

Date: _____

Symbol: _____   Company: _____

Opening Transaction

Transaction Recommended By _____

Why decision was made to do this transaction

Buy/Short	# of Shares	Price/share	Commission	Subtotal

Total opening transaction _____

Closing Transaction

Why decision was made to close at this price

Sell/cover	# of Shares	Price/share	Commission	Subtotal

Total closing transaction _____

Overall Profit/Loss _____

What I learned from this transaction

Date: _____

Symbol: _____   Company: _____

Opening Transaction

Transaction Recommended By _____

Why decision was made to do this transaction

Buy/Short	# of Shares	Price/share	Commission	Subtotal

Total opening transaction _____

Closing Transaction

Why decision was made to close at this price

Sell/cover	# of Shares	Price/share	Commission	Subtotal

Total closing transaction _____

Overall Profit/Loss _____

What I learned from this transaction

Date: _____

Symbol: _____ Company: _____

Opening Transaction

Transaction Recommended By
_____

Why decision was made to do this transaction

[   ]

Buy/Short	# of Shares	Price/share	Commission	Subtotal

Total opening transaction [   ]

Closing Transaction

Why decision was made to close at this price

[   ]

Sell/cover	# of Shares	Price/share	Commission	Subtotal

Total closing transaction [   ]

Overall Profit/Loss [   ]

What I learned from this transaction

[   ]

Date: _____

Symbol: _____   Company: _____

Opening Transaction

Transaction Recommended By
_____

Why decision was made to do this transaction

Buy/Short	# of Shares	Price/share	Commission	Subtotal

Total opening transaction _____

Closing Transaction

Why decision was made to close at this price

Sell/cover	# of Shares	Price/share	Commission	Subtotal

Total closing transaction _____

Overall Profit/Loss _____

What I learned from this transaction

Date: _____

Symbol: _____   Company: _____

Opening Transaction
Transaction Recommended By _____

Why decision was made to do this transaction

Buy/Short	# of Shares	Price/share	Commission	Subtotal

Total opening transaction _____

Closing Transaction
Why decision was made to close at this price

Sell/cover	# of Shares	Price/share	Commission	Subtotal

Total closing transaction _____

Overall Profit/Loss _____

What I learned from this transaction

Date: _____

Symbol: _____   Company: _____

Opening Transaction
Transaction Recommended By _____

Why decision was made to do this transaction

Buy/Short	# of Shares	Price/share	Commission	Subtotal

Total opening transaction

Closing Transaction
Why decision was made to close at this price

Sell/cover	# of Shares	Price/share	Commission	Subtotal

Total closing transaction

Overall Profit/Loss

What I learned from this transaction

Date: _____

Symbol: _____   Company: _____

Opening Transaction

Transaction Recommended By _____

Why decision was made to do this transaction

Buy/Short	# of Shares	Price/share	Commission	Subtotal

Total opening transaction _____

Closing Transaction

Why decision was made to close at this price

Sell/cover	# of Shares	Price/share	Commission	Subtotal

Total closing transaction _____

Overall Profit/Loss _____

What I learned from this transaction

Date: _____

Symbol: _____   Company: _____

Opening Transaction
Transaction Recommended By

Why decision was made to do this transaction

Buy/Short	# of Shares	Price/share	Commission	Subtotal

Total opening transaction _____

Closing Transaction
Why decision was made to close at this price

Sell/cover	# of Shares	Price/share	Commission	Subtotal

Total closing transaction _____

Overall Profit/Loss _____

What I learned from this transaction

Date: _____

Symbol: _____   Company: _____

Opening Transaction
Transaction Recommended By

Why decision was made to do this transaction

Buy/Short	# of Shares	Price/share	Commission	Subtotal

Total opening transaction _____

Closing Transaction
Why decision was made to close at this price

Sell/cover	# of Shares	Price/share	Commission	Subtotal

Total closing transaction _____

Overall Profit/Loss _____

What I learned from this transaction

Date: _____

Symbol: _____   Company: _____

Opening Transaction

Transaction Recommended By

Why decision was made to do this transaction

Buy/Short	# of Shares	Price/share	Commission	Subtotal

Total opening transaction

Closing Transaction

Why decision was made to close at this price

Sell/cover	# of Shares	Price/share	Commission	Subtotal

Total closing transaction

Overall Profit/Loss

What I learned from this transaction

Date: _____

Symbol: _____   Company: _____

Opening Transaction

Transaction Recommended By _____

Why decision was made to do this transaction

Buy/Short	# of Shares	Price/share	Commission	Subtotal

Total opening transaction _____

Closing Transaction

Why decision was made to close at this price

Sell/cover	# of Shares	Price/share	Commission	Subtotal

Total closing transaction _____

Overall Profit/Loss _____

What I learned from this transaction

Date: _____

Symbol: _____   Company: _____

Opening Transaction

Transaction Recommended By

Why decision was made to do this transaction

Buy/Short	# of Shares	Price/share	Commission	Subtotal

Total opening transaction _____

Closing Transaction

Why decision was made to close at this price

Sell/cover	# of Shares	Price/share	Commission	Subtotal

Total closing transaction _____

Overall Profit/Loss _____

What I learned from this transaction

Date: _____

Symbol: _____   Company: _____

Opening Transaction

Transaction Recommended By
_____

Why decision was made to do this transaction

_____

Buy/Short	# of Shares	Price/share	Commission	Subtotal

Total opening transaction _____

Closing Transaction

Why decision was made to close at this price

_____

Sell/cover	# of Shares	Price/share	Commission	Subtotal

Total closing transaction _____

Overall Profit/Loss _____

What I learned from this transaction

_____

Date: _____

Symbol: _____   Company: _____

Opening Transaction

Transaction Recommended By
_____

Why decision was made to do this transaction

Buy/Short	# of Shares	Price/share	Commission	Subtotal

Total opening transaction ☐

Closing Transaction

Why decision was made to close at this price

Sell/cover	# of Shares	Price/share	Commission	Subtotal

Total closing transaction ☐

Overall Profit/Loss ☐

What I learned from this transaction

Date: _____

Symbol: _____   Company: _____

Opening Transaction

Transaction Recommended By
_____

Why decision was made to do this transaction

Buy/Short	# of Shares	Price/share	Commission	Subtotal

Total opening transaction

Closing Transaction

Why decision was made to close at this price

Sell/cover	# of Shares	Price/share	Commission	Subtotal

Total closing transaction

Overall Profit/Loss

What I learned from this transaction

Date: _____

Symbol: _____   Company: _____

Opening Transaction

Transaction Recommended By

Why decision was made to do this transaction

Buy/Short	# of Shares	Price/share	Commission	Subtotal

Total opening transaction _____

Closing Transaction

Why decision was made to close at this price

Sell/cover	# of Shares	Price/share	Commission	Subtotal

Total closing transaction _____

Overall Profit/Loss _____

What I learned from this transaction

Date: _____

Symbol: _____   Company: _____

Opening Transaction

Transaction Recommended By _____

Why decision was made to do this transaction

Buy/Short	# of Shares	Price/share	Commission	Subtotal

Total opening transaction _____

Closing Transaction

Why decision was made to close at this price

Sell/cover	# of Shares	Price/share	Commission	Subtotal

Total closing transaction _____

Overall Profit/Loss _____

What I learned from this transaction

Date: _____

Symbol: _____   Company: _____

Opening Transaction
Transaction Recommended By

Why decision was made to do this transaction

Buy/Short	# of Shares	Price/share	Commission	Subtotal

Total opening transaction _____

Closing Transaction
Why decision was made to close at this price

Sell/cover	# of Shares	Price/share	Commission	Subtotal

Total closing transaction _____

Overall Profit/Loss _____

What I learned from this transaction

Date: _____

Symbol: _____   Company: _____

Opening Transaction

Why decision was made to do this transaction

Buy/Short	# of Shares	Price/share	Commission	Subtotal

Total opening transaction

Closing Transaction

Why decision was made to close at this price

Sell/cover	# of Shares	Price/share	Commission	Subtotal

Total closing transaction

Overall Profit/Loss

What I learned from this transaction

Date: _____

Symbol: _____   Company: _____

Opening Transaction

Transaction Recommended By
_____

Why decision was made to do this transaction

Buy/Short	# of Shares	Price/share	Commission	Subtotal

Total opening transaction [_____]

Closing Transaction

Why decision was made to close at this price

Sell/cover	# of Shares	Price/share	Commission	Subtotal

Total closing transaction [_____]

Overall Profit/Loss [_____]

What I learned from this transaction

Date: _____

Symbol: _____   Company: _____

Opening Transaction

Transaction Recommended By
_____

Why decision was made to do this transaction

Buy/Short	# of Shares	Price/share	Commission	Subtotal

Total opening transaction _____

Closing Transaction

Why decision was made to close at this price

Sell/cover	# of Shares	Price/share	Commission	Subtotal

Total closing transaction _____

Overall Profit/Loss _____

What I learned from this transaction

Date: _____

Symbol: _____   Company: _____

Opening Transaction

Transaction Recommended By

Why decision was made to do this transaction

Buy/Short	# of Shares	Price/share	Commission	Subtotal

Total opening transaction _____

Closing Transaction

Why decision was made to close at this price

Sell/cover	# of Shares	Price/share	Commission	Subtotal

Total closing transaction _____

Overall Profit/Loss _____

What I learned from this transaction

Date: _____

Symbol: _____   Company: _____

Opening Transaction
Transaction Recommended By _____

Why decision was made to do this transaction

Buy/Short	# of Shares	Price/share	Commission	Subtotal

Total opening transaction

Closing Transaction
Why decision was made to close at this price

Sell/cover	# of Shares	Price/share	Commission	Subtotal

Total closing transaction

Overall Profit/Loss

What I learned from this transaction

NOTES

Made in the USA
Monee, IL
31 October 2020